GIFTS FROM THE Garden

Mary Elizabeth
... paints beautiful little houses for your feathered friends.

Holly
... loves to give and receive big bouquets straight from the garden.

Kate
... made Ragweed potpourri for gifts last year.

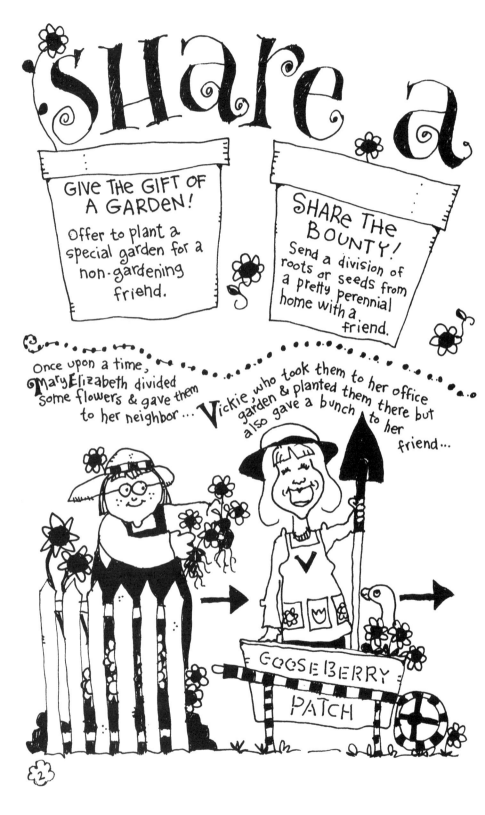

SHARE a

GIVE THE GIFT OF A GARDEN!

Offer to plant a special garden for a non-gardening friend.

SHARE THE BOUNTY!

Send a division of roots or seeds from a pretty perennial home with a friend.

Once upon a time, MaryElizabeth divided some flowers & gave them to her neighbor... Vickie, who took them to her office garden & planted them there but also gave a bunch to her friend...

GOOSEBERRY PATCH

garden

PLANT A MEMORY!
Give a tree or beautiful bush to commemorate a housewarming, anniversary or any special day.

BRIGHTEN A DAY!
Take bouquets from your yard to a local nursing home.

...Kate who got dirt in her eyes planting them so she gave the rest to her buddy...

...JoAnn, who couldn't squeeze one more flower in her garden...

...so she gave them to her neighbor Holly, who always has room for more.

Share a garden: Ideas!

- PLANT A POT OF HERBS FOR A COUNTRY FRIEND'S WINDOWSILL.

- MAKE SOMETHING DELICIOUS USING YOUR OWN HOME-GROWN GOODIES, AND SHARE IT WITH A BUDDY....

LIKE THIS YUMMY RECIPE:

apple S*N*A*P*S

* 3·½ LBS. APPLES, PEELED, CORED & SLICED
* 1 C. LEMON JUICE
* 4 C. WATER

* 2 C. SUGAR
* 1 C. BROWN SUGAR
* 2 T. CINNAMON

Pre-treat apple slices in lemon juice & water — soak fruit no longer than 10 minutes. Drain. Combine sugars & spice in large bowl. Put apples in sugar mixture. Dry in food dehydrator at 130° for 20 to 22 hours or until pliable. Turn halfway thru drying process.

I wonder if she'd like a few of these flowers for her garden....

Hmmm... wonder where she got those pretty flowers...

4

DIRTY WORK Coupon

I,

....

being of semi-sound mind and strong back, do hereby volunteer my services in your garden. This coupon may be redeemed for :

....

....

....

KATE GAVE A "WORK OF ART" TROWEL (see page 27) TO HOLLY ON HER BIRTHDAY WITH A COUPON FOR 1 LAWN-MOWING & 1 OVER-ALL WEEDING... chores that Holly abhors!

♥ COPY OUR COUPON FOR YOUR OWN DEVICES!

Volunteer for :

MULCHING   PLANTING
LAWN MOWING   HARVESTING
FERTILIZING   DIGGING HOLES
DIVIDING PLANTS   WEEDING
RE-POTTING   WATERING

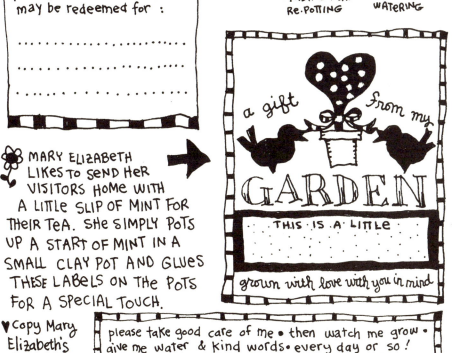

🌸 MARY ELIZABETH LIKES TO SEND HER VISITORS HOME WITH A LITTLE SLIP OF MINT FOR THEIR TEA. SHE SIMPLY POTS UP A START OF MINT IN A SMALL CLAY POT AND GLUES THESE LABELS ON THE POTS FOR A SPECIAL TOUCH.

♥ Copy Mary Elizabeth's Labels & color them, if you like, for your pot decorations!

a gift from my GARDEN

THIS IS A LITTLE ....

grown with love with you in mind

please take good care of me • then watch me grow • give me water & kind words • every day or so !

CARE INSTRUCTION:

Share a garden: ideas! more

wonderful Handmade Seed Packages.

Design your own seed packs to fill with seeds from your garden!

YOU MIGHT NEED:
- PAPER, PAPER BAGS, WRAPPING PAPER SCRAPS, THIN HANDMADE PAPERS
- RUBBER STAMPS
- PENS, MARKERS, COLORED PENCILS
- WATERCOLORS OR ACRYLIC PAINTS
- PAINTBRUSH, FINE-TIPPED
- GLUE STICK

GOOD PLANTS TO COLLECT SEEDS FROM:

BLACK-EYED SUSAN
CLEOME
COSMOS
MARIGOLD
PURPLE CONEFLOWER
SNAPDRAGON
ZINNIA
DILL
CILANTRO
BUTTERFLY WEED
COLEUS
GLOBE AMARANTH
MOONFLOWER
SALVIA
VINCA
SUNFLOWER
CHIVE

"She who shares the joy in what is grown spreads joy abroad & doubles his own."
~ anonymous ~

HOW TO BEGIN:

1. CUT A SEED PACKET TEMPLATE FROM A PIECE OF CARDBOARD ~ YOU ARE WELCOME TO USE OUR PATTERN ON THE OPPOSITE PAGE. USING A PENCIL, TRACE AROUND THE TEMPLATE ON THE WRONG SIDE OF THE DESIRED PAPER. CUT OUT.

2. DECORATE THE FRONT OF YOUR SEED PACKET- USE YOUR IMAGINATION ~ STAMP, COLOR & DRAW 'TIL YOU'RE SATISFIED!

3. TO PUT YOUR PACKET TOGETHER, FOLD SIDE (A) TO BACK. FOLD SIDE (B) OVER SIDE (A). SEAL CLOSED WITH GLUE STICK. (IT'S TRULY _EASY_ ~ DON'T LET THIS STEP SCARE YOU. EVEN KATE CAN DO IT.)

4. FOLD SIDE (C) UP OVER SIDE (A) & (B). SEAL CLOSED WITH GLUE STICK.

5. FILL WITH SEEDS. WRITE DIRECTIONS FOR PLANTING ON BACK OF PACKET.

★ FOR THOSE BUSY SOULS, ★
AN ALTERNATIVE:
ALMOST ★ HOMEMADE
SEED PACKETS

IF YOU LIKE THE IDEA OF SAVING YOUR
SEEDS FOR GARDEN GIFTS BUT JUST CAN'T FACE
FOLDING SIDE A OVER SIDE B, TAKE HEART;
HERE'S THE COUNTRY FRIENDS™ EASY OPTION—

GO TO THE STATIONERY OR OFFICE SUPPLY STORE. BUY
SOME LITTLE ENVELOPES. COPY OUR LABEL BELOW &
ENLARGE IT AS NEEDED OR TRIM OFF THE EXTRA
PARTS THAT WON'T FIT YOUR ENVELOPE. GLUE THE
LABEL ON & PUT SEEDS INSIDE. WHAT A CLEVER GIRL
YOU ARE! (ALL YOUR FRIENDS WILL THINK SO.)

Neighborly NOTES

Holly loves to
scout tag sales
for old teacups
to package with
her homemade seed packs.
She adds a little sack of
potting soil especially for
small containers and has
all the makings for a sweet
little fairy garden to give
to friends.

JoAnn tucks
in a little packet
of seeds when
she mails a
letter to a friend.

Kate is too "busy"
(i.e. too lazy) to save
seeds so she buys
pre-packed seeds in
bulk to   use in her
         packets.

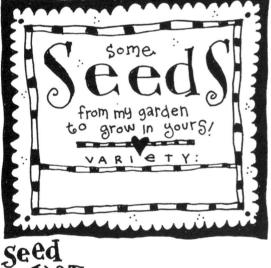

some Seeds
from my garden to grow in yours!
VARIETY:

Seed PACKET TEMPLATE

THIS IS THE TOP FLAP.

PACKET BACK (A)

(B)

(C)

ROCKET SCIENTIST

■ ■ ■ ■ FOLD LINES

━━━━ TRACING & CUTTING LINES

OH ♥ SO Sensational Strawberry Butter

homemade by your friend

✻ SPICY ✻ PEACH BUTTER

Homemade BY YOUR COUNTRY FRIEND

...a taste of summer goodness in every bite!

2 QTS. FRESH RIPE STRAWBERRIES
2 C. SUGAR
2 T. LEMON JUICE

Wash & clean berries. Crush berries with a potato masher. Place berries in a saucepan with no more than about ½ cup of water. Simmer slowly over low heat until strawberries are soft. Use a sieve or food mill to press cooked berries into a pulp. Measure out 5 cups of pulp and place in a clean saucepan. Mix in sugar & lemon juice. Let mixture stand 2 to 3 hours. Bring to a boil then reduce heat. To prevent mixture from sticking to pan, stir constantly as it thickens. Cook slowly 'til thick enough to round up on a spoon or to a spreading consistency. Ladle hot butter into hot jars. Be sure to leave ¼" headspace. Adjust 2-piece caps & process 10 minutes in a boiling water canner.

A GIFT FROM ME

HAPPY EATING!

✻ COPY THESE LABELS & GLUE 'EM ON!

...DELICIOUS ON MUFFINS

18 MEDIUM-SIZE PEACHES
4 C. SUGAR
1 t. CINNAMON
½ t. NUTMEG
½ t. GINGER

Blanch washed peaches in boiling water for ease in peeling. Peel, pit & chop fruit. Add no more than ½ cup of water to fruit in a saucepan. Cook until soft. Press cooked peaches through sieve or food mill. Measure out 2 quarts of peach pulp. In a large saucepan, combine pulp with sugar & spices. Cook 'til thick enough to round up on a spoon. Stir constantly to avoid sticking. Ladle into hot jars, leaving a ¼" headspace. Adjust 2-piece caps & process 10 minutes in a boiling water canner.

homemade Lazy Day Pickles

OPEN 'EM UP • EAT 'EM & THINK OF ME!

...PICKLES FRESH FROM THE FREEZER, NO CANNING NECESSARY!

3 LBS. CUCUMBERS, UNPEELED & THINLY SLICED

1 LARGE ONION, SLICED

2 MEDIUM GREEN PEPPERS, SEEDED, CORED & SLICED INTO RINGS

2 C. CIDER VINEGAR

2 C. SUGAR

¼ C. PICKLING SALT

1 T. MUSTARD SEED

1 T. CELERY

In a large bowl, combine cucumbers, onion & green pepper slices. Combine remaining ingredients in saucepan; bring to boil. Reduce heat ∾ simmer for 5 minutes. Pour over vegetables & let stand 30 minutes. Stir mixture occasionally. Evenly divide veggies & juice among freezer containers, allowing 1" headspace at top of each. Place covers on containers & freeze quickly. When ready to use, allow a day in refrigerator to defrost.

Home Made

*MMMMM*GOOD*
IF·I·DO·SAY·SO·MYSELF

YOU CAN **USE OUR LABELS** ON YOUR HOMEMADE CANNED GOODS & JAMS & JELLIES! JUST TAKE 'EM TO YOUR TRUSTY COPY MACHINE... RUN SOME COPIES. NOW RUN HOME, CUT 'EM OUT, COLOR 'EM WITH MARKERS IF YOU LIKE & GLUE 'EM ON! JUST FILL IN THE BLANKS, LIKE KATE DID ON HERS (BELOW). Hee Hee Hee

HOMEMADE BY KATE

THAT'S NOT FUNNY.

9

the Country Friends™ present

Always use fresh & healthy, ripe fruits. Rinse in clear water & drain. Unsweetened frozen fruit, thawed to room temperature, may also be used in recipes.

Be sure to wash jars in hot soapy water & rinse well. They should be free of nicks & cracks. Sterilize in boiling water for 10 to 20 minutes. To prevent jars from breaking when you ladle hot jam in, keep them in hot water 'til you need them.

Use regular, granulated sugar only! Don't use artificial sweeteners, sugar substitutes or sugar blends in recipes.

Never double recipes. You'll be doomed as mixtures will not set.

For best results & safety, process all jams & jellies following USDA recommended water bath method (page 13). Don't move processed jams & jellies around too much as this will affect the gel.

Wash & rinse all canning lids & bands. Lid may not be re-used. Prepare lids as directed by the manufacturer. Always wipe rim of jars before putting on lids & bands. Paraffin wax is no longer considered a safe method for sealing jams & jellies.

"JAM Tips

Your local Cooperative Extension Office is a good source for more information on canning jams & jellies. You can sometimes take canning workshops there, too!

Before storing jams & jellies, check seals on jars. The seals should be concave or curved down & stay that way when pressed on lightly. If it pops up the jam or jelly is not sealed. Wipe outside of jars before storing in dry, cool, dark spot. Use within 1 year.

11

Herbal Honey

START WITH PLAIN OLD HONEY... ADD A LITTLE OF THIS, A LITTLE OF THAT... A SWEET TREAT WILL "BEE" YOUR REWARD

Rosemary Honey

- 2.¼ c. HONEY
- 1 c. ROSEMARY, FINELY CHOPPED

PLACE HONEY & ROSEMARY INTO A PAN. HEAT SLOWLY OVER LOW HEAT FOR ABOUT ONE HOUR. POUR HONEY MIXTURE INTO 4-OUNCE JARS ~ LET SET 1 WEEK. DECORATE JARS WITH RAFFIA TIES & SPRIGS OF ROSEMARY.

Excellent in tea!

Hey, Look Honey!

Honey
especially for you from

TAKE THIS LABEL TO YOUR COPIER & MAKE SOME LABELS FOR YOUR HONEY JARS!

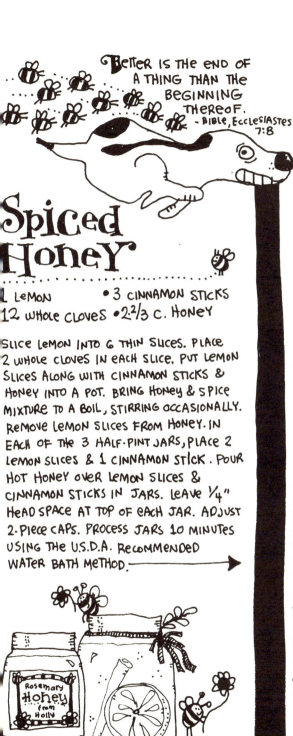

> "Better is the end of a thing than the beginning thereof."
> – Bible, Ecclesiastes 7:8

Spiced Honey

- 1 Lemon
- 12 whole cloves
- 3 cinnamon sticks
- 2 2/3 c. honey

Slice lemon into 6 thin slices. Place 2 whole cloves in each slice. Put lemon slices along with cinnamon sticks & honey into a pot. Bring honey & spice mixture to a boil, stirring occasionally. Remove lemon slices from honey. In each of the 3 half-pint jars, place 2 lemon slices & 1 cinnamon stick. Pour hot honey over lemon slices & cinnamon sticks in jars. Leave 1/4" head space at top of each jar. Adjust 2-piece caps. Process jars 10 minutes using the U.S.D.A. recommended water bath method. →

Rosemary Honey from Holly

INSP. KATE

To ensure the purity of your homemade honeys & to keep cooties out of your jams & jellies, follow these instructions:

In a canner or large saucepan of boiling water, place jars on a rack. The bottom of the glass jars should **NOT** come in contact with bottom of the pot. The water should cover the jars by 1 to 2 inches. Place lid on canner or pot & bring back to boil. Boil 5 minutes for smaller jars (8 ounce) & 10 minutes for larger jars (16 ounce). Remove jars. Let stand to cool. Check seals.

The garden is naturally filled with Old-Fashioned Beauty Secrets

Aaaah! Paradise! Were it not for the neighbors, Holly would just move the bathtub right out into the garden and while away the days!

Beauty without grace is a hook without bait. —NINON DE LENCLOS

a Refreshing Facial Steam

Observe yon handmaiden Kate preparing a spa treat from the herb garden for beloved Mistress Holly! (NOTE TO HANDMAIDENS: FACIAL STEAMS ARE NOT RECOMMENDED FOR VERY DRY SKINS, BUT ARE VERY REFRESHING FOR OTHER SKIN TYPES)

PLACE ABOUT 4 TABLESPOONS OF DESIRED HERBS IN A BOWL. BRING 5 CUPS OF WATER TO A ROLLING BOIL. POUR OVER HERBS. DRAPE A LARGE TOWEL OVER HEAD & SHOULDERS SO IT ENVELOPS THE BOWL FORMING A TENT. THIS WILL CATCH THE STEAM. BE SURE TO KEEP YOUR FACE AT LEAST A FOOT AWAY FROM THE STEAMING POT. AFTER STEAMING FACE FOR 5 TO 10 MINUTES (LIFT TOWEL EVERY SO OFTEN FOR A BREATH OF COOL, FRESH AIR), RINSE FACE WITH A COOL DAMP CLOTH. FOLLOW WITH A REFRESHING LOTION.

CHOOSE 1 OR MORE OF THESE HERBS FOR A FACIAL STEAM:

CALENDULA - all purpose skin herb

CHAMOMILE - slightly astringent

COMFREY - healing & slightly astringent

PEPPERMINT - healing, astringent & stimulating

ROSEMARY - good for oily skin

LAVENDER - helps refine pores, wonderful aroma

YARROW - very astringent, use for oily skin

Facial steams are NOT recommended for those who suffer from breathing or heart problems.

Ssssstt! Wanna Know

GROW A LUFFA!

PACK ONE IN A BASKET WITH RELAXING HERBAL BATH SALTS FOR A FAVORITE COUNTRY FRIEND.

SIMPLY FOLLOW THE DIRECTIONS ON A LUFFA GOURD SEED PACKET FOR PLANTING & GROWING. THEY GROW GREAT ON A TRELLIS! THE GOURD SHOULD BE ALLOWED TO RIPEN OFF THE VINE, TURNING FROM GREEN TO YELLOW. CUT GOURD OPEN & REMOVE SEEDS. STRIP OFF THE SKIN, WASH THE INSIDE FIBER & IT'S READY TO GO!

WHEN USED AS A BATH SPONGE, THE LUFFA WILL REMOVE OLD, DRIED SURFACE SKIN & LEAVE A HEALTHY GLOW... a wonderful gift from the garden.

YES   NO

PUFFY EYE CURE:

LAY DOWN & RELAX WITH A NICE, COLD SLICE OF CUCUMBER OVER EACH EYE FOR 10 TO 20 MINUTES. (CONTRARY TO KATE'S INSISTANCE, IT IS NOT EFFECTIVE TO PUT THE ENTIRE CUCUMBER OVER YOUR EYES.)

THE OLD **Lemon** TRICK: SIT WITH YOUR ELBOW IN THE "CUP" OF A LEMON HALF TO LIGHTEN DARK 5 O'CLOCK ELBOW SHADOW!

Promote a healthy glow on the outside, by filling up on the inside with lots of fruits & veggies

a Secret?
(A BEAUTY SECRET, THAT IS)

Lovely Lavender Vinegar

... NOT FOR COOKING BUT IT WILL GIVE YOU GOOD-LOOKING SKIN!

4 T. FRESH OR DRIED LAVENDER

1/4 C. FRESH MINT LEAVES

1½ C. CIDER VINEGAR

SPRING WATER

1. PLACE LAVENDER, MINT & VINEGAR IN CLEAR GLASS JAR.
2. COVER JAR WITH A NON-METAL LID — PUT IN A SUNNY SPOT FOR 2 TO 3 DAYS UNTIL VINEGAR TURNS A LOVELY SHADE OF LAVENDER.
3. STRAIN OUT HERBS.
4. MIX ½ CUP OF LAVENDER VINEGAR WITH 2 CUPS OF SPRING WATER IN A PRETTY BOTTLE. DECORATE WITH RIBBON & A SPRIG OF LAVENDER FOR A GREAT & GORGEOUS GIFT.

* (TRY THIS RECIPE WITH ROSEMARY, TOO — VERY SOOTHING!)

FOLK WISDOM

CARRY THE PIT OF AN AVOCADO WITH YOU TO PROMOTE BEAUTY.

DANCE AMONG FLAX PLANTS TO ENSURE BEAUTY IN ADULTS.

GINSENG WILL BRING LOVELINESS TO ALL WHO CARRY IT.

MAIDENHAIR FERN WORN ON THE BODY OR KEPT IN THE BED WILL GUARANTEE GRACE.

Beauty is in the heart of the beholder.

— AL BERNSTEIN —

paint a PAIL

FUN & EASY!

Begin with a plain old galvanized tin bucket, available at your trusty hardware store... large, medium or small, it's up to you!

STEP 1

Give your bucket a good going-over with a piece of medium sandpaper (This takes off the finish and will give your new paint something to "grab" onto.)

ZINNIA DAISY

GROW · G

STEP 2

You're ready to give the bucket a new base-coat of color. Using a sponge brush, apply a thin coat of flat acrylic paint (or any water-based paint) all over the pail's exterior. Let dry thoroughly according to paint instructions, then apply a second coat. You can also use a flat-finish spray paint ... but watch out for runs!

SUN SCREEN BALM

19

PAILS TO PAINT

STEP 3

Here's the fun part... you're ready to decorate the pail! Use your imagination or try Mary Elizabeth's ideas below ~ stencil or free hand a bold & colorful design using bright acrylic paints. Get going!

STEP 4

Okay! Now that your bucket is bright-and-beautiful and, of course, so cleverly decorated, seal your work with several coats of a clear varnish ~ spray it on, or use a sponge brush, letting your masterpiece dry thoroughly between coats.

PAILS: THE DETAILS

A FLOWER GARDEN
IN-A-PAIL

FILL IT UP WITH A BAG OF POTTING SOIL, A PACKAGE OF FERTILIZER, GARDEN GLOVES, A HAND-SHOVEL & A STACK OF SEED PACKS ~ DAISIES & ZINNIAS, OF COURSE!

Paint your pail a bright yellow. For the flowers, make a big black dot. Now, make a big, bold black circle around the dot ~ it'll look like this: Don't worry if it's kinda, sorta oblong or off-balance; that just makes it more interesting! Okay, now take pink or white (or whatever color you want) and make big old loopy petals, like this: ahead and add some plain old polka-dots on the pail, too ~ just for fun!

SUNSHINE PAIL

How about a plain old white paint job to begin? Once that's dry, jazz it up with a big swirl of gold. Remember those rays of golden sunshine! Voilá! There she shines!

YOUR GIFT BUCKET WILL SPARKLE WHEN FILLED WITH TREATS FOR A SUNNY DAY IN THE GARDEN: SUNSCREEN, AFTER-SUN BALM, SILLY SUNGLASSES & A BRIGHT YELLOW BALLHAT.

Vivid pink might be a good basecoat to start with! Paint a large red triangle, like so: Now, that's your strawberry. Dot on some "seeds" with a small brush or a cotton swab: Finish your berry by adding a star-shaped leaf on top; it might look like this.→ Speckle on some little red or green dots in between the berries to make it look lively!

BERRY BUCKET

YOUR BERRY BUCKET WILL MAKE A MUCH-LOVED GIFT FROM THE GARDEN WHEN YOU FILL 'ER UP WITH A PINK OR RED PLAID KITCHEN TOWEL TO LINE IT... A LOAF OF POUND-CAKE WRAPPED IN FOIL & TIED WITH A RED RIBBON... AND YOUR VERY OWN JAR OF HOMEMADE STRAWBERRY JAM! (OR JUST FILL IT WITH HOMEGROWN BERRIES RIGHT OUT-OF-THE-PATCH! mmmmm

You can never have too many Birdhouses

a neat gift!

...which is good 'cause Vickie has 743 at last count!
Birdhouses make a wonderful, whimsical gift for the garden...
whether it's a practical design or simply a decoration, the little
houses make a fun collection.

If you're planning to use your birdhouses to attract helpful,
insect-eating birds, keep in mind that one that's highly decorated
just might remain vacant. Get out your bird books ⌣ see which
birds like a big house, a small doorway, a certain roofline! Be a
good landlord and provide your feathered friends with a home sweet
home!

grow all sorts of interestingly-shaped Gourd BIRDHOUSES

Follow instructions on the back of a package of **BOTTLE GOURD SEEDS**. Bottle gourds grow very well on a trellis, and enjoy lots of water & sunlight. Cure your gourds by placing them on a wooden rack where air can circulate around them freely. Be sure to turn them occasionally. Gourds are dry when they turn brown, beige or cream & seeds rattle loosely inside. (It may take 3 to 6 months!)

To make a birdhouse from your gourd:

1. Wash gourd in soapy water to remove dirt & mold. Let dry. 2. Using a sharp knife or fine-toothed craft saw, cut a hole in the gourd's side 1" to 1½" in diameter. The size of the hole will determine which birds will "rent" your house. 3. Remove seeds & any remaining pulp. Clean inside with soapy water. 4. Attach a hanger & enjoy!

Hope is the thing with feathers that perches in the soul, and sings the tune without the words and never stops at all. ~ emily Dickinson

IF YOU DON'T WANT TO BE A BIRDIE LANDLORD, TRY YOUR HAND AT DECORATIVE

BIRDHOUSES

TO BRIGHTEN UP A ROOM OR FOR THE GREAT OUTDOORS!

THE BASICS:

SUPPLIES:
- Fine grade sandpaper
- acrylic or enamel paints
- paintbrushes - various sizes
- stencils (or use our patterns)
- water-based sealer if using acrylic paint
- Unfinished birdhouse
- An unbridled imagination!

1. IF USING ACRYLIC PAINTS, SAND BIRDHOUSE & SEAL WITH WATER-BASE ACRYLIC SEALER. PAINT BASE COAT.

2. FREEHAND YOUR DESIGN IN PENCIL IF YOU FEEL CREATIVE ∼ OR TRANSFER A DESIGN TO THE BIRDHOUSE BY THESE EASY STEPS:

Ⓐ TRACE DESIRED DESIGN ONTO TRACING PAPER.

Ⓑ TURN THE TRACING PAPER OVER NOW, AND ON THAT BACK SIDE BEHIND THE DESIGN, RUB WITH A PENCIL.

Ⓒ NOW LAY THAT PENCIL-RUBBING SIDE DOWN AGAINST YOUR PROJECT AND TRACE LIGHTLY AROUND THE DESIGN YOU MADE IN STEP Ⓐ. REMOVE THE PAPER ∼ YOU'VE TRANSFERRED THE DESIGN! NOW GET BUSY WITH YOUR PAINTS!

an idea:

KATE'S POKEY DOT PLACE

...just a frivolous figment of her fanciful mind!

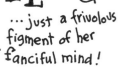

- Paint your birdhouse white.
- Now with a small-tipped paintbrush (or even a cotton swab will work for the manually unskilled), just put millions of polka dots all over the house. (Kate likes yellow & pink.)
- Around the bottom, paint on a wiggly line or two ∼ go all the way around. (Blue, perhaps?)
- You're done! A cheery place!

mary Elizabeth's Rosebud Cottage

... a pretty little idea.

- Basecoat your house a nice pale pink ∽ the roof cream.
- Draw skinny pink lines across the roof ∽ they don't have to be perfect! Squiggly stripes are fine!
- See the rosebud up here? ↗ You can either use tracing paper, or do an easy freehand rose like this ∽

① Paint a big dot of bright pink just like this:

② While that dot is still wet, dip a skinny brush in a deep red or burgundy paint and simply make a swirl on the pink dot:

③ Now add a slash of leaf-green paint to the side of the rose ∽ don't worry about the details ∽ we're looking for a Monet effect!

④ Just do rosebuds all over the walls of your birdhouse ∽ a charming cottage awaits you! (Hang it in your rose garden)

HOLLY's Sweet Dreams Motel
- early birds welcome!

Begin with a dark navy blue paint. Add many little white stars & a bright yellow moon... and don't be stingy with those stars! Paint on a whole universe of heavenly bodies in a variety of sizes. (you might even use glow-in-the-dark paint!)

z zzz zzz zzz

25

Violet & Pansy Bookmarks

Mary Elizabeth's favorite little flowers can be preserved in a thoughtful gift from the garden... a sweet reminder of summer bouquets all year long!

First, dry your flowers with this easy method:
1. Lay flowers & leaves between sheets of newspapers. Don't overlap!
2. Cover with heavy books for about 3 weeks.

Now, to make your bookmarks:
1. Arrange flowers & leaves on front of bookmark with tweezers. Tack into place with a small amount of craft glue.
2. Cover with a piece of wax paper ~ press until dry.
3. Cover with a piece of clear, self-adhesive vinyl contact paper.
4. Punch a hole at top of bookmark & add ribbon or silk cording.

She who kneels where violets grow a thousand secret things shall know.
—OLD FOLK RHYME

COUNTRY FRIENDS™ SUMMER POTPOURRI

½ c. ROSEBUDS
¼ c. ORANGE PEEL
¼ c. ROSE HIPS
¼ c. LAVENDER
¼ c. LEMON VERBENA LEAVES
¼ c. CHAMOMILE FLOWERS
¼ c. MARIGOLD FLOWERS

2 T. SUNFLOWER PETALS
2 T. ALLSPICE BERRIES
12 BABY BAY LEAVES
10 DROPS BERGAMOT OIL

5 DROPS SANDLEWOOD OIL
5 DROPS LEMONGRASS OIL
1 T. ORRIS ROOT

Combine all except oils & orris root in wide-mouth quart jar. Add orris root & oil & stir well. Place lid on jar - age for 2-3 weeks away from direct sun. Stir daily.

Kate's Work of ART
Garden Tools

...SO PRETTY, MAYBE YOU'LL LOOK FORWARD TO GARDEN CHORES.

YOU'LL NEED:
- enamel paints
- paintbrushes
- garden tools

HOW TO:
Paint tool handles with enamel paints in a solid color. Add stripes, squiggles & polka dots, bees, ladybugs...whatever! You're the artist!

*A WONDERFUL GIFT FOR A HOUSEWARMING OR A COUPLE'S SHOWER ~ A HAND-PAINTED HOE, SHOVEL & RAKE!

I ONLY **LOOK** LIKE I'M GOOFING OFF.

COUNTRY HARVEST P·O·T·P·O·U·R·R·I

- 1 c. WHOLE NUTMEGS, CRACKED
- 1 c. MINI INDIAN CORN
- 1 c. BEECH LEAVES
- 1 c. SMALL MAPLE, OAK OR ELM LEAVES
- 1 c. POPPY SEED HEADS
- 1 c. WHOLE MACE
- ½ c. CLOVES
- ½ c. CORIANDER SEEDS
- 1 t. PATCHOULI OIL
- 1 t. NUTMEG OIL

COMBINE ALL IN A GLASS JAR ~ SHAKE WELL. LET MIXTURE AGE FOR 2-3 WEEKS. SHAKE DAILY TO HELP BLEND FRAGRANCES.

JoAnn's Herbal Blends

Try JoAnn's delectable garden herb blends to spice up your everyday dishes. Fair warning, though: JoAnn likes her food **hot & snappy** ～ you may want to experiment with your blends to tone 'em down or go ballistic... it's up to you & your antacids!

STRONGLY- FLAVORED HERBS

BAY · GINGER · SAGE · ROSEMARY ～ use no more than 1 teaspoon for six · serving recipe.

Medium- flavored herbs

BASIL · CUMIN · DILL · FENNEL · TARRAGON · GARLIC · MARJORAM · MINT · OREGANO · THYME ～ use no more than 1 to 2 teaspoons for six - serving recipe.

Delicately- flavored herbs

BURNET · CHERVIL · CHIVES · PARSLEY ～ go crazy!

Poultry Seasoning

DRIED PARSLEY
GROUND ROSEMARY
DRIED ONION POWDER
DRIED SAGE LEAVES
GROUND MARJORAM
GROUND GINGER
(USE SPARINGLY)

Mix with a stick of butter & rub on outside of poultry.

Also delicious in herb breads & deviled eggs!

BBQ Blend

CHILI PEPPER
CUMIN SEED
OREGANO
GARLIC POWDER
SEA SALT (OPTIONAL)

SEAFOOD blend

BASIL
FRENCH TARRAGON
PARSLEY
BAY LEAF
LEMON THYME

Momma·Mia that's Italian

... delicious in pizza & spaghetti sauce!

DRIED MARJORAM LEAVES
DRIED BASIL
DRIED THYME
DRIED ROSEMARY
DRIED SAVORY
DRIED SAGE
DRIED OREGANO

ASK KATE:
YOUR CULINARY HERBAL QUESTIONS ANSWERED

Dear Kate: What exactly is Marjoram?

ANSWER: She's that nice elderly lady who lives next door to my aunt Edna.

Dear Kate: Where might I find Tarragon?

ANSWER: I believe it's west of France.

Dear Kate: Is Rosemary spicy?

ANSWER: No, ever since I've known her she's been very quiet & shy.

Dear Kate: Do you know anything about herbs & cooking?

ANSWER: Actually, no. Thank you.

* Please send your questions to Mary Elizabeth, the NEW answer person, in care of the Country Friends™.

Granny's Lavender

make a GARDEN MARKER

...so easy, the kids can make a bunch for gifts!

Simply choose some flat stones ⁓ paint herb & veggie names on them with enamels ⁓ and personalize them, too. They look great laying flat or standing up at the end of a garden row.

Did you Know...

...JoAnn is so organized she sets the Thanksgiving table 2 weeks before the holiday?

ORGANIZING IS WHAT YOU DO BEFORE YOU DO SOMETHING, SO THAT WHEN YOU DO IT, IT'S NOT ALL MIXED UP. - AA MILNE

Good-for-You Veggie Chips

RIPE TOMATOES	TURNIPS
CUCUMBERS	ZUCCHINI
YELLOW SQUASH	LIGHT-SEASONING SALT

CUT TOMATOES INTO ½" THICK SLICES. OTHER VEGGIES SHOULD BE CUT INTO ¼" THICK SLICES. ARRANGE IN SINGLE LAYER IN TRAYS OF DEHYDRATOR & SPRINKLE WITH SEASONING SALT. FOLLOW MANUFACTURER'S DIRECTIONS FOR DRYING. STORE IN REFRIGERATOR OR FREEZE IN PLASTIC CONTAINERS. SERVE WITH A DIPPING SAUCE.

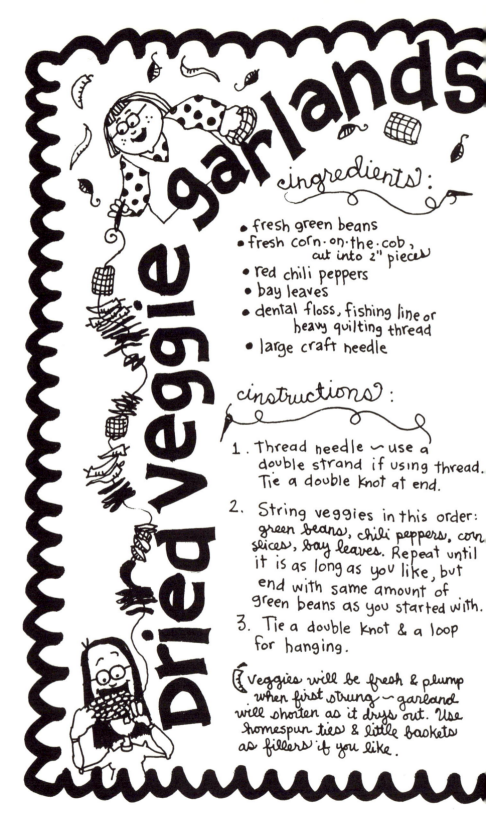

Dried Veggie garlands

ingredients:

- fresh green beans
- fresh corn·on·the·cob, cut into 2" pieces
- red chili peppers
- bay leaves
- dental floss, fishing line or heavy quilting thread
- large craft needle

instructions:

1. Thread needle — use a double strand if using thread. Tie a double knot at end.

2. String veggies in this order: green beans, chili peppers, corn slices, bay leaves. Repeat until it is as long as you like, but end with same amount of green beans as you started with.

3. Tie a double knot & a loop for hanging.

(Veggies will be fresh & plump when first strung — garland will shorten as it drys out. Use homespun ties & little baskets as fillers if you like.

Vickie can't bear to throw anything away ∽ She's a sentimental fool when it comes to, well, just about ANYTHING. If you're the same old softie as Vickie, here's a list of tips to turn your, uh, "treasures" into a goldmine of garden goodies:

★ that cracked <u>teacup</u> Aunt Bertha gave you can be planted with miniature roses....

★ Grandpa's old <u>metal toolbox</u> can be spruced up with a coat of enamel paint & filled with pots of herbs....

★ An ancient <u>wooden barrel</u> you've had in the garage since 1903 would look spiffy with a whitewash & a stenciled border & red geraniums....

★ Your <u>prom dress</u> can cloak a naked garden scarecrow....
(nothing personal! We're sure it was lovely!)

★ Kitchen herb gardens will thrive in rusty old <u>dishpans</u> you couldn't turn down at the neighbor's tag sale....

★ (we can't come up with any good uses for Vickie's junior high gym suit but we're working on it.)

junk goodies

Vickie's recycled

We are born of the earth, We return to the earth, and in between, We **garden.**

— old saying —

A WHOLE YEAR'S WORTH!

12 nice little gifts

from your

garden

JANUARY: A SMALL MUSLIN BAG FILLED WITH ORANGE PEELS & BITS OF GREENERY FROM YOUR CHRISTMAS TREE ...a lovely aroma!

FEBRUARY: 14 BRIGHT RED TULIP BULBS TO FORCE BY VALENTINE'S DAY.

MARCH: A SPRIG OF A FAVORITE HERB IN A BIODEGRADABLE PEAT POT... rosemary, perhaps?

APRIL: A SLICE OF HOMEMADE ANGELFOOD CAKE, DECORATED WITH THE SEASON'S FIRST VIOLETS!

MAY: JONQUILS IN AN OLD CANNING JAR. ADD AN ORGANDY RIBBON...PURPLE IS NICE!

JUNE: TENDER YOUNG ASPARAGUS, TIED INTO A BOUQUET WITH YELLOW STREAMERS...a fresh & tasty treat.

JULY: A BUCKET-FULL: 92 POUNDS OF ZUCCHINI!

AUGUST: A BOUQUET OF SAGE OR BASIL FROM THE HERB GARDEN.

SEPTEMBER: A BUSHEL OF SHINY JONATHAN APPLES.

OCTOBER: A PUMPKIN ALREADY CUT INTO A FRIENDLY-FACED JACK-O-LANTERN.

NOVEMBER: A JAR OF HOMEMADE SALSA FROM THE SUMMER'S TOMATO CROP.

DECEMBER: BAKED APPLES IN A PRETTY RED DISH, USING YOUR OWN ORCHARD'S HARVEST.